Foundations – Faith Life Essentials
Founded On The Rock

© 2009 Derek Prince Ministries–International
This publication DPM UK 2019

ISBN 978-1-78263-533-8
Product code: B100D

Scripture quotations are from the New King James Version of the Bible,
Thomas Nelson Publishers, Nashville, TN, © 1982.

This message is a transcript book with questions and study suggestions
added by the Derek Prince Ministries editorial team.

DPM
Derek Prince Ministries
www.derekprince.com

EXPANDED
VERSION:
GROUP
STUDY

Founded
on the
Rock

DPM

DEREK PRINCE MINISTRIES

Contents

About this Study Series...6

Founded on the Rock – an Introduction.......................................11

Part 1 - The Christian Life – A Building....................................15

Part 2 - Building on the Foundation...31

Part 3 - The Word of God..45

About the Author...61

About This Study Series

The Bible is God's Word and our "instruction manual" to find the path to salvation in Jesus. It then shows us how to walk with Him once we have come to know Him. Logically, therefore, it is a hugely important part of our challenge as Christian believers to study the Word of God.

A sad fact is that very often we forget most of what we have heard quite quickly! As a result, what we have heard often has little impact on the way that we continue to live.

That is why we developed these Study Guides. As Derek Prince has said numerous times in his teaching, "It is a general principle of educational psychology that children remember approximately 40 percent of what they hear; 60 percent of what they hear and see and 80 percent of what they hear, see and do."

This Study Guide is intended to help you to assimilate the truths that you have heard into both your head and into your heart so that they become more than just knowledge and will begin to change the way that you live.

Living the Christian life

This study is part of a series of 10 messages, based on the doctrinal foundation of the Christian life described in Hebrews 6:1-2 which says,

Therefore, leaving the discussion of the elementary principles of Christ, let us go on to perfection, not laying again the foundation of repentance from dead works and of faith

toward God, of the doctrine of baptisms, of laying on of hands, of resurrection of the dead, and of eternal judgment.

This mentions six specific foundation stones that we need to lay before we can build a dwelling place for the Lord in our hearts and lives:

1. Repentance from dead works
2. Faith towards God
3. The doctrine of baptisms – John's baptism, Christian baptism and baptism in the Holy Spirit
4. Laying on of hands
5. Resurrection of the dead
6. Eternal judgment.

When this teaching is applied in your life, with faith, we believe that it will deepen your relationship with God and enable you to live a truly successful Christian life.

How to Study

Each book contains a QR-code (or DVD) that links you to a talk by Derek Prince, the transcript of the talk and questions for personal application or to be discussed in a group setting.

Each video is about an hour long, divided in three parts. Set aside a reasonable length of time to read the Introduction, then watch or read Derek's teaching, and finally come back to the Study Guide to reflect on the Study Questions or to discuss them with your study group.

Once you have completed this series you will find that you have an excellent summary of the teaching. This will help you to share the content with others, whether to a friend, home group or congregation. The more you share the truths you are learning, the more they will become part of your own life and testimony.

Group Study

This study guide has been developed for use by small groups as well as by individuals.

Simply proceed through the material as a team, reflect on the questions and explore the statements together for a rich and rewarding experience.

Scripture to Memorize

In this book, we have chosen key Scriptures for memorization. They will relate in some way to your overall study. Memorizing them will place a spiritual sword in your hands which you, by the Holy Spirit, will be able to use in times of spiritual conflict.

The Word of God has supernatural power for those who will take the time and effort to "hide it in their hearts" by memorizing and meditating on it. As God's Word is hidden in your heart, it becomes constantly available to you for reference, comfort, correction and meditation. Put simply, it becomes part of your life.

Look up the verse in your own Bible and write it in the space provided. You will want to write and say this verse out loud several times until you are confident you know it well. Take time to meditate on the words and their application to your life. As a group, you could talk briefly about the meaning of the verse and its relevance to the lesson or share how you applied it.

You will be asked to recall your Memory Work at the end of the book.

Founded on the Rock – an Introduction

Founded on the Rock is the first message in the Foundation Series and is centered around the person of Jesus. Scripture tells us that there is no other foundation that can be laid other than the one that is already laid – Jesus Christ. Jesus is our personal foundation and before we start building, we need to ask ourselves two important questions:

1. What is my foundation – have I laid the right foundation?
2. Is my life built on Jesus – do I have a personal relationship with Him?

As Christians, we are responsible to build ourselves up as a dwelling place for the Lord and to do that we need to establish our lives on Jesus. In Matthew 16, starting at verse 13, Jesus asks His disciples the same question that He asks each of us today – "Who do you say that I am?"

As you study this teaching, ask God to reveal to you the state of your spiritual foundation and how you can establish it more firmly in Jesus.

Watch the Derek Prince video teaching *Founded on the Rock* on YouTube. Scan the QR-code or visit dpmuk.org/foundations

This video has been divided into three sections, following the chapters in this book. You will find the links to these sections when you tap the 'down arrow' to expand the information about the video.

Write down these verses and try to memorize them.

John 17:3

AND THIS IS LIFE ETERNAL, THAT THEY MIGHT KNOW THEE THE ONLY TRUE GOD AND JESUS CHRIST WHOM THOU HAST SENT.

John 14:23

JESUS ANSWERED AND SAID UNTO HIM IF A MAN LOVE ME HE WILL KEEP MY WORDS AND MY FATHER WILL LOVE HIM AND WE WILL COME UNTO HIM AND MAKE OUR ABODE WITH HIM.

MEDITATION

You cannot build a more
successful Christian life
than your foundation
will permit.

The Christian Life
- A Building

The Bible is a model of good teaching and it follows various principles. One in particular is that it starts from the known to lead people on to the unknown. It never starts with the unknown, it starts with what is known and proceeds from there to the unknown. One of the ways the Bible does this is to take very simple, familiar, everyday experiences and activities and give them a spiritual application. There are various examples. The Bible speaks about a farmer sowing his seed, about a fisherman catching fish in a dragnet or a soldier putting on his armor. In a completely different kind of context, it speaks about a bride preparing herself for her wedding. Those are just a few examples of this principle.

The particular, familiar activity I want to focus on is that of constructing a building. This picture of the Christian life is used at least as many times as any other picture in the Bible. We are going to turn, first of all, to the epistle of Jude, which is a word of exhortation to us as believers.

> But you, beloved, building your selves up on your most holy faith, praying in the Holy Spirit, keep yourselves in the love of God.
> Jude 20–21

Scripture says here that we must build ourselves up in our most holy faith. It is one of the ways in which this metaphor of building applies. We are responsible to build ourselves up. Then in Ephesians 2 it speaks about a holy temple in the Lord:

...in whom the whole building, being fitted together, grows into a holy temple in the Lord, in whom you also are being built together for a dwelling place of God in the Spirit.
Ephesians 2:21–22

Speaking about the collective Christian community, we are to be built together in the Holy Spirit as a place for God to dwell. Then, speaking about Jesus as a living stone, Peter says:

Coming to Him [Jesus] as to a living stone, rejected indeed by men, but chosen by God and precious, you also, as living stones, are being built up a spiritual house, a holy priesthood, to offer up spiritual sacrifices acceptable to God through Jesus Christ.
1 Peter 2:4–5

There we are compared, each one of us, to living stones that are being built together into a holy temple that the Lord is going to occupy. Let's look at one final example from Acts 20. It is the farewell of Paul to the Ephesian elders whom he loved with a special love because it was in Ephesus that his ministry had perhaps the greatest impact of any other place. In his speech in Acts 20, Paul is saying farewell and telling them they will never see him again in this life. It was a very moving situation for all of them. This is really the final exhortation he wanted to leave with them:

So now, brethren, I commend you to God and to the word of His grace, which is able to build you up and give you an inheritance among all those who are sanctified.
Acts 20:32

Paul is telling us that the main means for building us up is the word of God's grace, the Bible. He says it is able to build us up and to give us an inheritance among all those who are set apart for Jesus Christ by faith in Him.

The Foundation Is Jesus

I am not a builder, but I know one thing: In any permanent building, whether it is built of brick or stone, concrete or timber, the vital area is the foundation. The Bible deals specifically with this, and it is an issue of great importance for every one of us. The foundation sets limits to the building that may be built above it—both in size and in weight. The foundation sets the limits, and this also is true in the Christian life. You cannot build a more successful Christian life than your foundation will permit. This is the vital issue: What is your foundation? Have you laid the right foundation? There is only one foundation that is adequate and all-sufficient. It is the person of Jesus Christ. Paul, writing to the Corinthian Christians, uses two metaphors. He uses the agricultural metaphor but then goes on to use the building metaphor.

> *For we are God's fellow workers* [working together with God]; *you are God's field* [that is the agricultural metaphor and] *you are God's building* [that is the construction metaphor]. *According to the grace of God which was given to me, as a wise master builder* [Greek, "architect"] *I have laid the foundation, and another builds on it. But let each one take heed how he builds on it. For no other foundation can anyone lay than that which is laid, which is Jesus Christ.*
> *1 Corinthians 3:9–11*

Paul says there is only one foundation for the Christian life and that is Jesus Himself. Anything that is not built on that foundation will not stand the test of time and of trial. So, it is very important for every one of us to assess what our life is built on. Are we truly built on the Lord Jesus Christ? Do we have a personal relationship and a knowledge of Jesus that makes us able to relate personally to Him? The question of laying this foundation in Jesus is extremely important, so I want to take some time to deal with the issue of how we can have this foundation—the foundation of Jesus—in our lives. I would invite each reader to examine his or her own life—your spiritual condition and spiritual experience—and check as to whether your relationship with the foundation is right. Let's begin in Matthew 16 with some basic teaching. Jesus is talking to His disciples:

> When Jesus came into the region of Caesarea Philippi, He asked His disciples, saying, "Who do men say that I, the Son of Man, am?" So they said, "Some say John the Baptist, some Elijah, and others Jeremiah or one of the prophets." [Then He makes it very personal.] He said to them, "But who do you say that I am?" Simon Peter answered and said, "You are the Christ [Messiah], the Son of the living God." Jesus answered and said to him, "Blessed are you, Simon Bar-Jonah, for flesh and blood has not revealed this to you, but My Father who is in heaven. And I also say to you that you are Peter, and on this rock I will build My church, and the gates of Hades shall not prevail against it."
> Matthew 16:13–18

This was a crucial moment in the life of Peter and in the whole history of Christianity. Jesus used this encounter with Peter to establish the way in which we can lay a foundation in Jesus Christ Himself. It has often been suggested that Peter is the foundation of the Church. I would have to say, if it were so it would be a very wobbly building—because a little later Jesus rebukes Peter by saying, "Get behind Me, Satan" (Matthew 16:23). Later still, Peter denied the Lord three times (John 18:15–17, 25–27). Even after the resurrection Paul had to rebuke him for compromising with the truth of the gospel for fear of his fellow Jews. (See Galatians 2:11–16.)

I, for one, am grateful that the Church is not built on Peter—nor on me! What actually emerges from this passage, which is very clear in the Greek testament (which is the original version that we have), "You are Peter [petros], and on this rock [petra] I will build My church" (Matthew 16:18). *Petros* in Greek means a stone or at most a boulder, nothing bigger than that. Normally it would be the kind of stone that people would take up to stone someone with. On the other hand, *petra* means a jagged rock that extends from the bedrock. It is often used to describe a cliff or something on that scale.

The important thing to remember is, it is part of the bedrock. What is the bedrock? It is just what Peter had been going through: the recognition of Jesus for who He is, revealed only by the Holy Spirit. No one can know Jesus and who He really is unless God the Father by the Holy Spirit reveals Him. This is the petra—it is the bedrock on which our Christian faith must be based. It is a personal encounter and a personal revelation of Jesus—not as the carpenter's Son, not as a historical figure, but as the eternal, uncreated Son of God.

That is where we have to come if we are going to build on that rock. The experience through which Peter passed must be paralleled in our experience. I have told people many times, "You can join a church, you can go through a religious ceremony, or you can say a prayer and still not be changed. But if you really encounter Jesus, you will be changed. No one encounters Jesus and remains the same." Each of us needs to ask:

Have I ever had this life-changing, personal encounter with the Lord Jesus Christ?

Encountering Jesus

I would like to suggest four successive phases through which Peter passed in his encounter of Jesus.

First of all, *confrontation*. Jesus and Peter met face to face. There was no mediator, no priest, no one between them. It was a direct, personal confrontation of Jesus. That is what our experience should be, too. Jesus said in another place, "I am the door. If anyone enters by Me, he will be saved" (John 10:9). There is only one way into the kingdom of God— through the door. The door is not a church; it is not a doctrine; it is Jesus. "I am the door."

Second, the confrontation was followed by *revelation*, a revelation granted by God the Father through the *Holy Spirit*. Jesus said, "Flesh and blood has not revealed this" (Matthew 16:17). You cannot arrive at it by your natural senses, there has to be a revelation. This is essential. No one can know Jesus as He truly is in His eternal Sonship of God without a personal revelation. You can study theology, you can go to a Bible college, you can even become a minister. But without this personal revelation of Jesus, you cannot know Him. The revelation comes only from God the Father through Jesus Christ the Son. Have you had that personal encounter with Jesus? I have. More than fifty years ago in the middle of the night in an Army barrack room during World War II, I encountered Jesus. I had no doctrinal knowledge, no evangelical language. I could not even say I was "saved" or "born again." I learned all that later. But I was changed— radically and permanently changed. I was not made perfect—in fact, let me confess to you, I am still not perfect. But I was changed for the better.

The third step is, there has to be an *acknowledgment* of what the Holy Spirit shows us. We have to say, "Yes, I believe. I receive." We have to make some kind of response. It is not automatic; it requires something happening in us.

And fourth, there has to be a *public confession* of our faith in Jesus. That is what Jesus drew out of Peter: "You are the Christ [Messiah]" (Matthew 16:16). Peter made it public. People speak about "secret believers," and I acknowledge there are secret believers, especially in countries where acknowledgement of that fact would mean being put to death. But nobody can permanently remain a secret believer, for Jesus said:

> *Therefore, whoever confesses Me before men, him I will also confess before My Father who is in heaven. But whoever denies Me before men, him I will also deny before My Father who is in heaven.*
> *Matthew 10:32–33*

Jesus in His characteristic way does not give us three choices, only two. We either confess or we deny. If we fail to confess in an appropriate situation, we are, in effect, denying. So, each one of us at some point has to come to the place where we openly acknowledge our faith in the Lord Jesus Christ. This is a critical moment for many. I discovered in the army after I had become a believer that the best thing to do was to let everybody know the first moment you met them where you stand. Then you never have to go back and say, "I didn't really tell you at the beginning, but…" So, I did something every night in the barrack room, which is not just a religious act. Wherever I was, I would kneel down at my bed and pray. That revealed just what kind of person they were dealing with. It was much easier that way. I saw other Christians who waffled, who did not come right out and say what they believed, and it was much harder for them to go back afterwards and make the right confession. I want to recommend that practice. We do not have to stand on a street corner and preach, we do not have to be a teacher. We can be housewives or students, but wherever we are, we should let people know we believe in Jesus, that He is the Son of God.

Let me just review those four successive phases of this encounter, which is so basic. This is how we lay the foundation of Jesus in our lives personally.

First, there was a confrontation.
Second, there was a revelation granted by God the Father through the Holy Spirit.
Third, Peter responded with an acknowledgment.
And fourth, he made a public confession.

What About Today?

The question might arise: is such a revelation possible today? Is it possible for people like you and me to know Jesus just as genuinely and just as personally as Peter and the other disciples did? We need to see two important things.

First of all, Jesus was not revealed to Peter as the Son of the carpenter. He had known Him that way for quite a while. Jesus was revealed to Peter as the eternal Son of God. The Scripture says in Hebrews 13:8:

Jesus Christ is the same yesterday, today and forever.

There has been no change in Him; there never will be. So, it is not a question of language, culture or clothing, but it is a question of the eternal person of Jesus. That is what Peter encountered; maybe for the first time in his life. Peter really had a revelation of who Jesus is.

Second, the revelation was granted through the Holy Spirit. The Bible calls the Holy Spirit the eternal Spirit, the timeless Spirit. Time, fashion, history, customs, language— they do not change the Holy Spirit.

For those two reasons it is equally possible for you and me to have this direct, personal revelation of Jesus, just as it was possible for Peter. First of all, because it is the eternal Son of God who is revealed; and secondly, because it is the eternal Spirit who reveals Him.

MY NOTES

MY NOTES

Study Questions

1. What special insights did you gain from this lesson?

    ----

2. Jude 20-21 exhorts us to do three things:
    - Build ourselves up in our faith
    - Pray in the Holy Spirit
    - Keep ourselves in the love of God.

    What does 'building yourself up in your faith' mean to you? Based on the three things listed in Jude 20-21, can you give examples as to how you do that?

    ----

3. See Jude 20-21; Ephesians 2:22; 1 Peter 2:4-5; Acts 20:32. According to God's Word, your spiritual life isn't static, it should be growing and developing. Why could it be important to build yourself up in your faith?

    These verses show that your spiritual growth is not just an individual issue, but that it's also important for your church and the Church worldwide. How does this reality make you feel?

    ----

4. Read Acts 20:32. What is the main means for building you up? Describe the role of God's Word in your daily experience.

    ----

5. According to 1 Corinthians 3:9-11, Jesus Himself is the only foundation for the Christian life. What does this mean?

----

6. Today, as in Peter's encounter with Jesus, there are four successive stages in order to lay this foundation:
    - A personal confrontation between Jesus and the person, without any mediator.
    - A revelation, granted by the Father, through the Spirit, about Jesus, the Son.
    - To acknowledge what the Holy Spirit shows about Jesus.
    - A public confession of your faith in Jesus, with the mouth.

    When you have been raised in a Christian family, these successive stages may not be as obvious as when someone from a non-Christian background becomes a believer. Whatever your situation, reflect on these stages and describe or discuss which ones you recognise. How did God work in your life?

----

7. In Matthew 16:13–18, Jesus asks, "But who do you say that I am?" Peter's response to that question highlights some important facts in Jesus' use of the words petros (stone or boulder) for Peter and petra (a big crag or cliff – a necessary part of the bedrock) for Himself. We must each ask ourselves this question: Are we built on a boulder or on the bedrock? How would you know?

----

8. Derek Prince encourages us to let people know we believe in Jesus, that He is the Son of God. In fact, he says: "If we fail to confess in an appropriate situation, we are, in effect denying Jesus." How do you feel about this? How do you feel about sharing your faith publicly? Can you give examples from your own life where you made it known to people that you were a believer? Pray for God to give you more creativity and boldness to publicly confess your faith.

----

9. Take time to thank God for what you have learned during this section. Ask Him to help you apply the teaching so your faith will grow, and so He will be manifested in your life, for His glory.

SUMMARY

- In the Bible, the Christian life is compared to a building. We must build ourselves up in our most holy faith and we are to be built together in the Holy Spirit as a place for God to dwell. (Jude 20-21, Ephesians 2:21-22)

- The main means for building us up is the Word of God's grace, the Bible. (Acts 20:32)

- There is only one foundation for the Christian life and that is Jesus Himself. Anything that is not built on that foundation will not stand the test of time and of trial. (1 Corinthians 3:9-11)

- There are four successive phases to lay the foundation of Jesus in our lives (see Matthew 16:13-18):
  - A personal confrontation with Jesus Christ.
  - A revelation granted by God the Father through the Holy Spirit.
  - An acknowledgement of what the Holy Spirit revealed about Jesus.
  - A public confession of our faith in Jesus Christ.

The Christian life is
not a storm-free life.

Building on
the Foundation

We come now to the next important practical issue: if we have laid the foundation, how do we proceed to build on it? You remember that the metaphors we cited at the beginning of this study all spoke about building. So the next vitally important and practical issue is how to build on the foundation. For this, I want to look at a well-known parable of Jesus—a parable about the wise man and the foolish man. Each of them built a house, but they built it different ways.

> *Therefore whoever hears these sayings of Mine, and does them, I will liken him to a wise man who built his house on the rock* [the bedrock, petra]: *and the rain descended, the floods came, and the winds blew and beat on that house; and it did not fall, for it was founded on the rock. But everyone who hears these sayings of Mine, and does not do them, will be like a foolish man who built his house on the sand: and the rain descended, the floods came, and the winds blew and beat on that house; and it fell. And great was its fall.*
> Matthew 7:24–27

First of all, it is important to see that each house was subjected to the same test. Neither house was free from being tested. The same storm that hit one house hit the other. The Christian life is not a storm-free life. We will go through storms. God has never guaranteed that we will not. In fact, Paul and Barnabas said to the early Church, "We must through many tribulations enter the kingdom of God" (Acts 14:22). If we are on a road that has no tribulation, it is questionable whether it leads to the kingdom of God, because that is what Paul said. It is not in the scope of this message to explain why we go through tribulation but, believe me, God has a purpose in it. If someone is going through it now, don't give up. God will bring you through and you will find at the end that He has dealt with you and taught you things you could not learn any other way. I know that from personal experience. The wise man builds in two ways: by hearing and doing the words of Jesus, the words of the Bible.

How can we build on the foundation? In just the same way: by hearing what the Bible says and doing it. We cannot be just a hearer only, because the Bible has no promises for them, but only for the hearer and doer. It is practical. It is applying the teaching of the Bible and the teaching of Jesus in our own lives. We find as we go on in this that God will continually open up new areas in which we need to apply the truth. I have been a Christian now for more than fifty years, but God is continually showing me new ways in which to apply His Word—new areas of my life in which I need to apply it. My building is not complete; it is still being built. But I thank God it has passed through a number of storms successfully.

Dig Deep

Another parable of Jesus is very similar, but there is an important addition. Jesus says:

> But why do you call Me 'Lord, Lord,' and do not do the things which I say?
> Luke 6:46

That is an important question. It is futile to call Jesus "Lord" if you do not obey Him, because the very title means someone who is to be obeyed. Jesus wants us to beware of just having a vocal confession that does not affect the way we live. He goes on:

> *Whoever comes to Me, and hears My sayings and does them, I will show you whom he is like: He is like a man building a house, who dug deep and laid the foundation on the rock. And when the flood arose, the stream beat vehemently against that house, and could not shake it, for it was founded on the rock* [the bedrock, the petra]. *But he who heard and did nothing is like a man who built a house on the earth without a foundation, against which the stream beat vehemently; and immediately it fell. And the ruin of that house was great.*
> *verses 47–49*

There is one important detail added in Luke which is not in Matthew. I wonder how many noticed it? It says the man who wanted to reach the bedrock had to dig deep. He had to get a lot of things out of the way before he could build on the bedrock.

That is also true with many of us. For most of us who grew up in a nominal Christian culture, there are a lot of hindrances and influences we must get out of the way before we reach the bedrock. Others who have grown up in a completely non-Christian culture will have to eliminate things, too, but they will be different. I want to suggest five hindrances that we need to dig out of the way.

Tradition

Now, not all traditions are bad. Some are good. We do not want to throw out all tradition. However, Jesus said to the people of His day, "You have made the commandment of God of no effect by your tradition" (Matthew 15:6). Even if we believe in traditions and act on them, it does not mean they are in line with the Scripture. According to my observation, Jesus would say exactly the same thing to the same

Jewish people today. "By your traditions you have made the Word of God of no effect." But let's not just look at the Jews. This is also true of many others of Christian backgrounds. We have inherited traditions, ways of acting, things we do, words we speak, which are not necessarily in line with Scripture. So we must be very careful to check these out.

Prejudice

The second hindrance we need to eliminate is prejudice. There is really no one who has not had some prejudice at one time or another. There are all sorts of prejudices, such as racial prejudices. Unfortunately, the world is full today of racial prejudices. We know in countries like South Africa, for instance, where racial prejudices eliminated certain people from being part of the Church (where there has been a wonderful change, let me add). A terrible thought! But that is not the only area where there is racial prejudice.

The United States of America has been full of racial prejudice and in many places still is today. I am from a British background so I know the British people have their prejudices, too. I grew up with many of them. I have had to dig deep to get rid of them. My own family background is from India. All my forbears served with British forces in India. I remember as a boy of about twelve saying innocently at a lunch, "I don't see why you couldn't invite an Indian to lunch." The reaction was one of horror in my family. I thought, What is the reason for this? Well, later on I realized that is prejudice. Believe me, no matter what your racial background is, very few people are free from all racial prejudice.

There is denominational prejudice. Most of us react in a somewhat negative way to certain denominations. My first wife Lydia, who is with the Lord, was Danish. She grew up in the Danish Lutheran Church and then she did something that was terrible in their eyes. She was baptized as a believer—which they call in Danish "a second-time baptizer." In her case, because she was a teacher in the Danish state school system, she actually went before the Parliament so they could ascertain whether or not she could remain a teacher. Lydia continued to have a denominational prejudice with the Lutheran Church really to the end of her days. I do not justify that; I believe it was a weakness in her. When I hear about people belonging to a certain denomination, I develop an attitude against them without ever having met them. I think, Well, they're going to be like that, and this is where they're wrong" and so on. Experience has taught me, if possible, that I should never judge a person till I have met them. I have met people from "wrong" denominational backgrounds who are some of the most "right" people I know. Also some who were from the "right" background who were wrong. So we must not give in to denominational prejudice.

Then there is social prejudice. Again, I am an example of somebody brought up with social prejudice, but I was not even aware of it. I just didn't know how the rest of the world lived. I was educated in Britain at Eton and then at Cambridge University. Then I got plunged into the British Army and I was together with all sorts of people I never had been together with. I began to realize how limited my knowledge of my own British people was. I thank God for that experience, five and a half years in the British Army; it cleansed me of a lot of social prejudices. Having been from a family of officers, I was used to being on that level, and when I was not on that level I learned something. When you see people from the same level, they look one way. But when you see them from below they look different. I have always tried to be sensitive to this, with the Lord's help.

There is also personal prejudice. Some people do not like others who have loud voices. Some people do not like people with red hair. There are all sorts of silly, personal prejudices most of us have. I have a prejudice against people who munch apples. I really fight it, but the prejudice is still there in the background because I just don't like that noise.

Preconception

The third hindrance to get out of the way are preconceptions. For instance, some people have a completely false view of who Jesus is: gentle Jesus, meek and mild, turning up at the Christmas party. That is not the real Jesus. He was a very different kind of person, very shocking, and prone to eliminate our prejudices and preconceptions. There are many other ways we can have preconceptions.

For instance, preconceptions of what it would be like to be a Christian. Growing up, I thought to myself, If I were to become a Christian, it would mean misery for the rest of my life. Like Pat Boone, I thought, Heaven isn't worth seventy years of misery on earth! so I completely eliminated the possibility of being a Christian—until I met Jesus.

Unbelief

A fourth hindrance—and something that is very dangerous—is unbelief. Sometimes when I am going to teach I will begin by getting everyone to renounce unbelief, because many of us are still beset by unbelief in various areas. Our minds are not really open to faith.

Rebellion

Lastly, and I think the most important, is rebellion. We might say, "I'm not a rebel." Oh, yes, we are! And if we have not yet discovered it, we will go on being one. Every descendant of Adam is born with a rebel inside. We have to identify that rebel and deal with it. God has only got one remedy for the rebel—and that is execution! God does not send the rebel to church; He does not teach him the Golden Rule; and He does not have him memorize Scripture. God puts him to death! But the mercy of God is, the execution took place nearly two thousand years ago when Jesus died on the cross. "Our old man was crucified with Him" (Romans 6:6). We have to come to the place where we identify that rebel inside us and willingly submit to execution.

Study Questions

1. What special insights did you gain from this lesson?

    ----

2. Read Matthew 7:24-27. List two things you need to do to build your faith on Jesus.

    ----

3. The Christian life is not a storm-free life. Reflect on Deuteronomy 8:2-3 and Acts 14:22. Write down/discuss your thoughts.

----

4. Read Luke 6:46.
    *   When and why do you call Jesus 'Lord'?

    ----

    *   What does it mean that Jesus is Lord?

    ----

    *   What practical applications are there, to calling Jesus Lord?

    ----

5. Reflect/discuss: The Bible has no promises for hearer only, but only for the hearer and doer. (See Luke 6:49)

----

6. What 'foundations' other than Christ can people build their lives upon?

    ----

7. Reflect/discuss: In order to construct a building of any good size or permanence, we need to dig deep, and dispose of those things that hinder our spiritual growth.

    ----

8. Derek Prince suggests five hindrances that we need to dig out of the way in order to build our lives on Jesus.
    *   Traditions. What are your favorite traditions? In what way do they bring you closer to God? Are there traditions that are hindering you from following Jesus?

        ----

    *   Prejudice. Derek lists examples like racial, denominational, social and personal prejudices. Can you give examples of a prejudice

you had towards others, or that you have experienced from others? Ask God to reveal any prejudice in your heart. Repent if the Holy Spirit convincts you of something.

- Preconceptions, about God, following Jesus, the Church, being a Christian. Do you recognize this in your life?

- Unbelief. Satan's oldest trick is to make us doubt God's love, promises and provision. Ephesians 6 exhorts us to take the shield of faith, with which we an extinguish all the flaming arrows of the evil one. Often, Christians feel ashamed to honestly share about their doubts, fears and unbelief. But bringing it in the light and asking God for forgiveness and help. Renouncing your unbelief and confessing your faith out loud is in fact a way to beat the enemy. Take some time to do so now.

- Rebellion. Derek says: You're a rebel. Do you recognize this to be true in your life? What does it mean to you that your 'old man was crucified with Christ'?

----

9. Take time to thank God for what you have learned during this section. Ask Him to help you apply the teaching, so your faith will grow and He will be manifested in your life, for His glory.

SUMMARY

- Jesus Christ is the only foundation for the Christian life. He is Lord. We build on the foundation of our faith by hearing what the Bible says and doing it. (Matthew 7:24-27)

- We must get rid of the hindrances and influences that get in the way of us building on the bedrock (Jesus), such as:
  - Tradition
  - Prejudice
  - Preconception
  - Unbelief
  - Rebellion.

We do not love God
more than we love
His Word.

The Word of God

Now I come to the Bible because this is as important as anything else in the Christian life. What is our attitude to the Bible? Is it the same as that of Jesus? I just want to take one passage of John's gospel. Jesus said:

> *If He [God] called them gods, to whom the word of God came*
> *(and the Scripture cannot be broken)...*
> *John 10:35*

This is a very significant verse because in it Jesus uses the two main titles for the Bible: the "Word of God" and "the Scripture." When He calls the Bible "the Word of God," it means that it proceeded from God, not from man. It may have come through human channels, but it is a word that comes from God. The phrase "the Scripture" is a limiting phrase. It means that which has been set down in writing. God has said many things which are not set down in writing. But by divine overruling the Bible contains those things God said that He saw needed to be set down in writing. That is the Scripture—that which is written.

Concerning that, Jesus made one, simple, sweeping statement: "The Scripture cannot be broken." We can argue as much as we like about the inspiration of the Bible or the authority of the Bible, but Jesus has said it all: It cannot be broken. It is absolutely authoritative. It will be totally fulfilled. Everything in it will be exactly worked out.

We can take a stand against it and deny it, but we cannot break it. In fact, if we deny it, ultimately it will break us. The Scripture cannot be broken.

There is a type of study called "higher criticism," which subjects the Scriptures to all sorts of ridiculous fantasies and ends up by making it a totally ineffective book. If there is one thing the devil wants to do in our lives, it is to undermine our faith in the authority and accuracy of the Bible. But, if we are like Jesus, we simply say, "The Scripture cannot be broken."

Jesus Is the Word

Not only is the Bible the Word of God, but Jesus Himself is the Word of God. This comes out in John's gospel in two places:

In the beginning was the Word, and the Word was with God, and the Word was God.
John 1:1

And the Word became flesh and dwelt among us, and we beheld His glory, the glory as of the only begotten of the Father, full of grace and truth.
John 1:14

That refers to Jesus. He was the Word, He is the Word. When Jesus was born, the Word became flesh. But He always was the Word. Eternally He was the Word with God. When He comes back, how is He coming back? What will His name be? This is a picture of Jesus coming out of heaven in glory to establish His kingdom on earth.

Now I saw heaven opened, and behold, a white horse. And He who sat on him was called Faithful and True, and in righteousness He judges and makes war. His eyes were like a

flame of fire, and on His head were many crowns [diadems,
royal crowns]. *He had a name written that no one knew
except Himself. He was clothed with a robe dipped in blood,
and His name is called The Word of God.*
Revelation 19:11–13

This is truly remarkable in the sense that when He first came He was
the Word, and when He comes back He will be the Word. He always
was the Word, still is the Word and will be the Word. That brings out
something very important. There is total agreement between Jesus
and the Bible. Our attitude toward one is the attitude toward the
other. We cannot believe in Jesus and disbelieve the Bible. Can we
absorb that fact? Jesus is the Word of God—He is the Word made
flesh. The Bible is the Word in Scripture, or in writing. Our attitude
toward the one must be the same as our attitude toward the other.
There is total agreement between the two.

Five Vital Facts

I would now like to examine five vital facts about the Word of God
and our relationship to it, which are contained in John's gospel, in
just three verses. Jesus is, in a sense, taking farewell of His disciples.
He is warning them that He is about to leave and they will be left on
their own for a while. It is a very traumatic time for the disciples; they
are overwhelmed with this revelation. But in the middle of it, Jesus
gives a marvelous revelation of what the Bible should mean to us as
believers. He says:

*A little while longer and the world will see Me no more,
but you will see Me. Because I live, you will live also.*
John 14:19

Jesus made a distinction there between the world—those who do
not acknowledge Jesus—and His own disciples. He said the world

would not see Him but the disciples would. Then Judas asked Him a very relevant question:

> *Judas (not Iscariot) said to Him, "Lord, how is it that You will manifest Yourself to us, and not to the world?"*
> *verse 22*

The answer Jesus gave is just full of important truth.

> *Jesus answered and said to him, "If anyone loves Me, he will keep My word; and My Father will love him, and We will come to him and make Our home with him."*
> *verse 23*

I want to bring out five vitally important facts in the answer of Jesus.

First of all, Jesus said He would reveal Himself to His disciples, not to the world. What is the distinguishing mark between the disciples and the world? The answer is keeping the Word of God. True disciples keep the Word of Jesus. They are not marked out by denominational labels; they are marked out by the way they relate to the Word. That is what makes us, or otherwise prevents us, from being true disciples. It is our relationship to the Word of God.

Keeping God's Word distinguishes disciples from the world. In every congregation every one of us is in one or other of those two categories. If we are disciples, we keep the Word of God. If we do not keep the Word, we belong to the world—the world that is not under the Lordship of Jesus. The second truth is, Jesus said, "If anyone loves Me, he will keep My Word." So, keeping God's Word is the supreme test of the disciple's love for God. Love is the motivation for obedience.

It is very important to understand that, as believers, we are not motivated by fear; we are motivated by love. In a certain sense, the Law used the motivation of fear: "If you do this, you will be punished." But that does not work. I have helped to raise a large number of children. I discovered that while children are under your control as a parent, you can use fear—but once they leave you, if they were motivated by fear, they will change. The only motivation that will keep them loyal and faithful is love. God and Jesus were wise enough not to build on fear but to build on love. Keeping God's Word is the supreme test of the disciple's love for God. Love is the motivation for obedience.

Then Jesus says, "If anyone loves Me, he will keep My Word, and My Father will love him." That is another wonderful fact. Keeping God's Word is what causes God the Father to love us with a special love. God loves the whole world in a certain way. But God has a very different degree and kind of love for true disciples of Jesus, for those who keep His Word. Looking back to the question that Judas asked, "How is it that You will manifest Yourself to us, and not to the world?" we see Jesus' answer was, "If anybody loves Me, he will keep My Word." So, how does Christ manifest Himself to us? Through the Word. It is through the keeping of the Word that we get to know Jesus better.

We could perhaps have some wonderful, spiritual experience—being caught up to the third heaven or something. But that does not happen to most people and it is not the basic way by which God reveals Himself and Jesus reveals Himself. It is through keeping the Word of God. Finally, and this is an amazing statement: "If anyone loves Me . . . My Father will love him, and We will come to him and make Our home with him."

There are only a very few places in the Bible where the plural pronoun is used about God, but this is one of them. Jesus says We—My Father and I—will come to him and make our home with him. That is a breathtaking statement, an amazing revelation that God the Father and God the Son want to come and make their dwelling with us. They want to make us their personal abode. But how does it come about? Through the Word. If we are not lovers of the Word, if we are not obedient to the Word, God will not make His dwelling place with us.

Let me say this as I close, and it is a very solemn thought: We do not love God more than we love His Word. So if we want to know how much we really love God, how much place God has in our life, we can find out. It is not something we need to speculate about. Just ask yourself these questions: How much do I love the Bible? How much place does the Bible have in my life? Because that is as much as you love God and that is as much place as you give to God in your life.

Let me summarize those five statements about the Bible because they are crucial. So many Christians are in a kind of twilight zone, they do not really know what is light and what is darkness. They wish and they hope, but they are not really sure. It is because they have not given the Word of God its rightful place in their lives.

1. Keeping God's Word distinguishes true disciples from the world.

2. Keeping God's Word is the supreme test of the disciple's love for God. Love is our motivation for obedience, not fear.

3. Keeping God's Word is the supreme cause of God's love for the disciple. God loves disciples in a special way. He loves the whole world, but He has a special love for disciples. But, those whom He loves as disciples are those who keep God's Word. If we want to be specially dear to God, then we have to keep His Word.

4. Through God's Word, kept and obeyed, Christ manifests Himself to us. The question was, "How will You manifest Yourself to us, and not to the world?" Jesus said, "If you love Me, you will keep My Word. That is how I will manifest Myself."

5. Finally, through God's Word, the Father and the Son will come together to indwell us. That is an amazing thought that just takes my breath away. God the Father and God the Son want to make their dwelling with us. But they will only do it as we keep God's Word.

Heavenly Father, thank You for Your Word—the Word of God, the Bible. This sure, authoritative, infallible Word is a lamp for our feet and a light for our path. I pray, Lord, for everyone who ultimately is confronted by this message, that You will cause us to be lovers of Your Word. That You, by Your grace, will enable us to give Your Word, the Bible, its rightful place in our lives that we may be truly disciples of the Lord Jesus.

Study Questions

1. What special insights did you gain from this lesson?

    ----

2. If there is one thing the devil wants to do in our lives, it is to undermine our faith in the authority and accuracy of the Bible. One of the ways he tries to do so is through liberal theology and science like "higher criticism". Can you think of other examples from culture (media, science, etc) or from personal experience, of how the devil is trying to make people doubt God's Word? How should we respond? (try not to give a general answer, but to be specific and practical.)

    ----

3. Jesus said that Scripture cannot be broken. He confirmed and trusted the authority and trustworthiness of the Bible. Is your attitude the same as that of Jesus? How does His attitude towards the Bible impact yours, for instance; does it raise questions or does it strengthen your hope?

----

4. Reflect/discuss: We cannot believe in Jesus and disbelieve the Bible.

----

5. Your attitude to the Bible is your attitude towards Jesus. If you neglect the one, you neglect the other. Derek Prince says, you don't love God more than you love His Word. Would you agree? Why (not)? Ask yourself, "How much do I love the Bible? How much place does the Bible have in my life?"

----

6. John 14:19,22-23 contains five vital facts about the Bible, the Word of God:

- Keeping God's Word distinguishes true disciples from the world. If we are disciples, we keep the Word of God. If we do not keep the Word, we belong to the world.
- Keeping God's Word is the supreme test of the disciple's love for God – Love is the motivation for obedience.
- Keeping God's Word is the supreme cause of God's love for the disciple.
- Through God's Word, kept and obeyed, Christ manifests Himself.
- Through God's Word, the Father and the Son together indwell the disciple.

  Consider these five facts. Is there one that stands out for you? Why?

  Consider the others: in how much do they apply to you?

----

7. As believers, we are not motivated by fear to obey God's Word; we are motivated by love. Yet, too often, Christians mix their love for Christ and their trust in God's grace with trying to earn God's righteousness by obeying His commands. They tend to mix grace and law. Ask the Lord to reveal if there is any 'mix' in your heart and if so, repent from it. Take time to thank God for His grace through Jesus Christ.

----

8. As you finish this study, let's reiterate the question Jesus asks all His disciples – "Who do you say that I am?" Has your answer changed as you have listened to this message?

Pray and ask for God's help to apply the truths from this study practically in your life. Remember to thank God for every new revelation that He shows you and to receive it with gladness. Here is a prayer to help you:

PRAYER

Dear Lord, thank you for helping me to establish my spiritual life on the bedrock of Jesus. As I build, I ask that You would help me to be both a hearer and a doer of Your Word, the Bible.

I want to dig deep and remove all the obstructions to a solid foundation: negative traditions, prejudices, preconceptions, unbelief and rebellion. Often I can't see these things in my own life even though they are so close – reveal them to me and show me the tools I must use to dig them out.

Help me to regularly test my attitude to the Bible, recognizing that my attitude to Your Word shows my attitude to You. Continue to teach me through Your Word and Your Holy Spirit. Amen.

SUMMARY

- Jesus said the Scripture cannot be broken. It is absolutely authoritative. It will totally be fulfilled. We should have the same attitude towards the Bible as Jesus has.

- Jesus was the Word from the beginning, He still is the Word and will be the Word when He comes back. There is total agreement between Jesus and the Bible. We cannot believe in Jesus and disbelieve the Bible.

- Five vital facts about the Word of God and our relationship to it: (John 14:19,22-23)
  - Keeping God's Word distinguishes true disciples from the world.
  - Keeping God's Word is the supreme test of the disciple's love for God.
  - Keeping God's Word is the supreme cause of God's love for the disciple
  - Through God's Word, kept and obeyed, Christ manifests Himself.
  - Through God's Word, the Father and the Son together indwell the disciple.

In the next study, *Authority and Power of God's Word*, you will examine your relationship with God's Word, the many ways Jesus' life fulfilled Scripture and the effects God's Word can have in your life.

Recall and write down the verses you memorized
at the beginning of this book:

John 17:3

John 14:23

About the Author

Derek Prince (1915–2003) was born in India of British parents. He was educated as a scholar of Greek and Latin at Eton College and King's College, Cambridge in England. Upon graduation he held a fellowship (equivalent to a professorship) in Ancient and Modern Philosophy at King's College. Prince also studied Hebrew, Aramaic, and modern languages at Cambridge and the Hebrew University in Jerusalem. As a student, he was a philosopher and self-proclaimed agnostic.

Bible Teacher

While in the British Medical Corps during World War II, Prince began to study the Bible as a philosophical work. Converted through a powerful encounter with Jesus Christ, he was baptized in the Holy Spirit a few days later. Out of this encounter, he formed two conclusions: first, that Jesus Christ is alive; second, that the Bible is a true, relevant, up-to-date book. These conclusions altered the whole course of his life, which he then devoted to studying and teaching the Bible as the Word of God.

Discharged from the army in Jerusalem in 1945, he married Lydia Christensen, founder of a children's home there. Upon their marriage, he immediately became father to Lydia's eight adopted daughters – six Jewish, one Palestinian Arab, and one English. Together, the family saw the rebirth of the state of Israel in 1948. In the late 1950s, they adopted another daughter while Prince was serving as principal of a teacher training college in Kenya.

In 1963, the Princes immigrated to the United States and pastored a church in Seattle. In 1973, Prince became one of the founders of Intercessors for America. His book Shaping History through Prayer and Fasting has awakened Christians around the world to their responsibility to pray for their governments. Many consider underground translations of the book as instrumental in the fall of communist regimes in the USSR, East Germany, and Czechoslovakia.

Lydia Prince died in 1975, and Prince married Ruth Baker (a single mother to three adopted children) in 1978. He met his second wife, like his first wife, while she was serving the Lord in Jerusalem. Ruth died in December 1998 in Jerusalem, where they had lived since 1981.

Teaching, Preaching and Broadcasting

Until a few years before his own death in 2003 at the age of eighty-eight, Prince persisted in the ministry God had called him to as he traveled the world, imparting God's revealed truth, praying for the sick and afflicted, and sharing his prophetic insights into world events in the light of Scripture. Internationally recognized as a Bible scholar and spiritual patriarch, Derek Prince established a teaching ministry that spanned six continents and more than sixty years.

He is the author of more than fifty books, six hundred audio teachings, and one hundred video teachings, many of which have been translated and published in more than one hundred languages.

He pioneered teaching on such groundbreaking themes as generational curses, the biblical significance of Israel, and demonology. Prince's radio program, which began in 1979, has been translated into more than a dozen languages and continues to touch lives. Derek's main gift of explaining the Bible and its teaching in a clear and simple way has helped build a foundation of faith in millions of lives. His nondenominational, nonsectarian approach has made his teaching equally relevant and helpful to people from all racial and religious backgrounds, and his teaching is estimated to have reached more than half the globe.

DPM Worldwide Ministry

In 2002, he said, "It is my desire – and I believe the Lord's desire – that this ministry continue the work, which God began through me over sixty years ago, until Jesus returns." Derek Prince Ministries International continues to reach out to believers in over 140 countries with Derek's teaching, fulfilling the mandate to keep on "until Jesus returns." This is accomplished through the outreaches of more than thirty Derek Prince offices around the world, including primary work in Australia, Canada, China, France, Germany, the Netherlands, New Zealand, Norway, Russia, South Africa, Switzerland, the United Kingdom, and the United States.

For current information about these and other worldwide locations, visit **www.derekprince.com.**

FOUNDATIONS
faith life essentials

www.dpmuk.org/shop

This book is part of a series of 10 studies on the foundations of the Christian faith.

Order the other books to get everything you need to develop a strong, balanced, Spirit-filled life!

1. Founded on the Rock

There is only one foundation strong enough for the Christian life, and we must be sure our lives are built on Jesus Himself.

2. Authority and Power of God's Word

Both the Bible and Jesus Christ are identified as the Word of God. Learn how Jesus endorsed the authority of Scripture and how to use God's Word as a two-edged sword yourself.

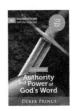

3. Through Repentance to Faith

What is faith? And how can you develop it? It starts with repentance: to change the way we think and to begin acting accordingly.

4. Faith and Works

Many Christians live in a kind of twilight - halfway between law and grace. They do not know which is which nor how to avail themselves of God's grace.

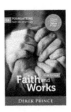

5. The Doctrine of Baptisms

A baptism is a transition - out of an old way of living into a totally new way of living. All of our being is involved. This study explains the three different forms of baptism presented in the Bible.

6. Immersion in the Spirit

Immersion can be accomplished in two ways: the swimming pool way and the Niagara Falls way. This book takes a closer look at the Niagara Falls experience, which relates to the baptism of the Holy Spirit.

7. Transmitting God's Power

Laying on of hands is one of the basic tenets of the Christian faith. By it, we may transmit God's blessing and authority and commission someone for service. Discover this Biblical doctrine!

8. At The End of Time

In this study, Derek Prince reveals the nature of eternity and outlines what lies ahead in the realm of end-time events.

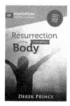

9. Resurrection of the Body

The death and resurrection of Jesus produced a change in the universe. Derek explains here how the resurrection of Jesus impacted man's spirit, soul, and body.

10. Final Judgment

This book examines the four major, successive scenes of judgment in eternity. Exploring the distinctive aspects of these four judgments, Derek opens the Scriptures to bring forth treasures hidden there.

Christian Foundations Course

If you have enjoyed this study and would like to deepen your knowledge of God's Word and apply the teaching – why not enrol on Derek Prince's Christian Foundations Bible Course?

Building on the Foundations of God's Word

A detailed study of the six essential doctrines of Christianity found in Hebrews 6:1-2.

- Scripture-based curriculum
- Practical, personal application
- Systematic Scripture memorisation
- Opportunity for questions and personal feedback from course tutor
- Certificate upon completion
- Modular based syllabus
- Set your own pace
- Affordable
- Based on *Foundational Truths for Christian Living*

For a prospectus, application form and pricing information, please visit www.dpmuk.org, call 01462 492100 or send an e-mail to enquiries@dpmuk.org

Foundational Truths For Christian Living

Develop a strong, balanced, Spirit-filled life, by discovering the foundations of faith: salvation; baptism, the Holy Spirit, laying on hands, the believers' resurrection and eternal judgment.

Its reader-friendly format includes a comprehensive index of topics and a complete index of Scripture verses used in the book.

ISBN 978-1-908594-82-2
Paperback and eBook
£ 13.99

www.dpmuk.org/shop

More best-sellers by Derek Prince

- Blessing or Curse: You can Choose
- Bought with Blood
- Life-Changing Spiritual Power
- Marriage Covenant
- Prayers & Proclamations
- Self-Study Bible Course
- Shaping History Through Prayer and Fasting
- Spiritual Warfare for the End Times
- They Shall Expel Demons
- Who is the Holy Spirit?

For more titles: www.dpmuk.org/shop

Inspired by Derek's teaching?

Help make it available to others!

If you have been inspired and blessed by this Derek Prince resource you can help make it available to a spiritually hungry believer in other countries, such as China, the Middle East, India, Africa or Russia.

Even a small gift from you will ensure that that a pastor, Bible college student or a believer elsewhere in the world receives a free copy of a Derek Prince resource in their own language.

Donate now: www.dpmuk.org/give
or visit www.derekprince.com

Derek Prince Ministries

DPM–Asia/Pacific
38 Hawdon Street
Sydenham
Christchurch 8023
New Zealand
T: + 64 3 366 4443
E: admin@dpm.co.nz
W: www.dpm.co.nz

DPM–Australia
15 Park Road
Seven Hills
New South Wales 2147
Australia
T: +61 2 9838 7778
E: enquiries@au.derekprince.com
W: www.derekprince.com.au

DPM–Canada
P. O. Box 8354 Halifax
Nova Scotia B3K 5M1
Canada
T: + 1 902 443 9577
E: enquiries.dpm@eastlink.ca
W: www.derekprince.org

DPM–France
B.P. 31, Route d'Oupia
34210 Olonzac
France
T: + 33 468 913872
E: info@derekprince.fr
W: www.derekprince.fr

DPM–Germany
Söldenhofstr. 10
83308 Trostberg
Germany
T: + 49 8621 64146
E: ibl@ibl-dpm.net
W: www.ibl-dpm.net

DPM-Netherlands
Nijverheidsweg 12
7005 BJ, Doetinchem
Netherlands
T: +31 251-255044
E: info@derekprince.nl
W: www.derekprince.nl

Offices Worldwide

DPM–Norway
P. O. Box 129
Lodderfjord
N-5881 Bergen
Norway
T: +47 928 39855
E: sverre@derekprince.no
W: www.derekprince.no

Derek Prince Publications Pte. Ltd.
P. O. Box 2046
Robinson Road Post Office
Singapore 904046
T: + 65 6392 1812
E: dpmchina@singnet.com.sg
W: www.dpmchina.org (English)
 www.ygmweb.org (Chinese)

DPM–South Africa
P. O. Box 33367
Glenstantia
0010 Pretoria
South Africa
T: +27 12 348 9537
E: enquiries@derekprince.co.za
W: www.derekprince.co.za

DPM–Switzerland
Alpenblick 8
CH-8934 Knonau
Switzerland
T: + 41 44 768 25 06
E: dpm-ch@ibl-dpm.net
W: www.ibl-dpm.net

DPM–UK
PO Box 393
Hitchin SG5 9EU
United Kingdom
T: + 44 1462 492100
E: enquiries@dpmuk.org
W: www.dpmuk.org

DPM–USA
P. O. Box 19501
Charlotte NC 28219
USA
T: + 1 704 357 3556
E: ContactUs@derekprince.org
W: www.derekprince.org

Lightning Source UK Ltd.
Milton Keynes UK
UKHW050047150720
366461UK00005BA/146